Hidden No More

A God-Centered Path to Freedom from Pornography

By Dr. Caleb Perkins

Scripture quotations are taken from the **English Standard Version (ESV®)**.

Cover Design: Abby Perkins

ISBN: 979-8-9946105-3-4

Printed in the United States of America.

TABLE OF CONTENTS

Author's Note

This book was written with care, prayer, and restraint.

Pornography is a deeply personal subject, and for many, even approaching it can stir fear, hesitation, or shame. Some worry they will be judged. Others fear exposure. This book is not written to confront you with condemnation or demand disclosure. It is written to create a safe space for honesty, reflection, and healing.

The intent of this book is pastoral. It avoids graphic detail and sensational language intentionally. You will not be asked to relive experiences or confess specifics. Instead, you are invited to understand formation, identity, and alignment in a way that leads toward freedom without fear.

This book does not assume why you are reading it. You may be here for personal growth, leadership, discipleship, or to support someone you love. Wherever you are, you are welcome to proceed at your own pace. Nothing in these pages requires perfection. Growth is measured by awareness, not performance.

If you read this book alone, that is enough. If you read it in community, let that space be marked by confidentiality, grace, and maturity. If you need to pause or return later, that is not a sign of failure. It is wisdom.

Healing begins with safety. God is present with you, not waiting on you. You are not defined by struggle, but by identity. As you read, take what is helpful and allow truth to unfold gently.

You are not alone.
You are not disqualified.
You are invited into the light without fear.

Stepping Into the Light

There are struggles people confess easily and struggles they hide carefully. Some sins are spoken aloud in prayer circles, counseling rooms, and testimonies. Others remain unspoken, locked behind silence, fear, and shame. Pornography belongs to the second category.

Throughout my years of military service and ministry, I have observed a quiet battle taking place behind disciplined lives, strong leadership, and sincere faith. Men and women who love God, who serve faithfully, who lead families and organizations, yet privately wrestle with something they do not know how to name without fear of judgment. Pornography is rarely discussed openly, not because it is uncommon, but because it is deeply personal and profoundly isolating.

This book exists because silence has proven costly.

We live in a culture saturated with technology. Phones, tablets, and computers are constant companions, tools we rely on for work, communication, and connection. Technology itself is not the enemy. It is a tool, morally neutral, shaped by how it is used. Yet embedded within this accessibility is unprecedented exposure to explicit content.

What previous generations had to seek out deliberately is now available instantly, privately, and endlessly.

Pornography does not discriminate. It affects men and women, the married and unmarried, the young and the old. Despite age verification prompts and disclaimers, access is largely unrestricted. With a single click, content is available to anyone willing to look. Early exposure is common. Repetition is easy. Secrecy is almost guaranteed.

Many assume the primary problem is that people are unwilling to talk about it. In reality, many are desperate to talk about it. The deeper issue has often been the reluctance of spiritual leadership to address it with clarity, courage, and compassion. Where discipleship remains silent, shame fills the gap. Where instruction is absent, people attempt to fight private battles with public expectations. This disconnect produces exhaustion, not freedom.

Pornography is often treated as a behavior problem. Stop doing this. Avoid that. Try harder. While behavioral strategies have a place, they are insufficient on their own. Behavior is rarely the root. It is the fruit of something deeper. Identity, desire, formation, and intimacy all play a role. Addressing pornography without addressing the heart is like pruning branches while ignoring the soil.
The psychological effects of pornography are well-documented. Repeated exposure stimulates dopamine and

endorphin release, training the brain to associate arousal with novelty, secrecy, and instant gratification. Over time, this desensitizes the mind. What once shocked no longer satisfies. Escalation becomes common, not because desire grows, but because sensitivity diminishes. This neurological pattern does not make someone weak. It makes them human. Understanding this matters because shame thrives where understanding is absent.

The physical and relational effects are equally significant. Unrealistic expectations distort intimacy. Desire becomes disconnected from the relationship. Some experience decreased drive toward real connection, preferring the ease of solitary release over the vulnerability of shared intimacy. Others struggle with performance anxiety or emotional distance. These effects often produce confusion and discouragement, especially within marriage, where intimacy was designed to flourish.

Yet the deepest impact of pornography is spiritual.

Pornography offers gratification without covenant, pleasure without presence, intimacy without responsibility. It mimics a connection while hollowing it out. Spiritually, it trains the heart to seek fulfillment apart from relationship, to consume rather than to commune. Over time, it reshapes posture before God.

God does not abandon His people when they struggle. Scripture consistently reveals a God who draws near to the broken, the tempted, and the weary. However, when struggles are hidden, something shifts internally. Like Adam and Eve in the garden, shame introduces hiding. Not hiding from God's location, for He is omnipresent, but hiding from His awareness. The posture of hiding dulls sensitivity to His presence. It creates distance in experience, not in reality.

This is why pornography feels spiritually numbing. Not because God has withdrawn, but because shame has altered awareness.

The purpose of this book is not to condemn, expose, or embarrass. It is to bring things into the light where healing becomes possible. Freedom does not begin with stricter rules. It begins with honest alignment. Before behavior changes, perception must change. Before habits are broken, identity must be restored.

Breaking free from pornography is not about promising God you will never fail again. That approach relies on willpower, and willpower alone is fragile. True repentance is not merely feeling sorry or making vows in moments of resolve. Biblical repentance is a transformation of thinking. It is asking the Holy Spirit to renew how we see God, how we see ourselves, and how we see others.

People are not objects of consumption. They are image bearers. The person on a screen is someone's son or daughter, created in the likeness of God. Availability does not equal permission. Desire must be trained, not indulged. Scripture consistently teaches that what we behold shapes who we become.

This book will address boundaries, accountability, and practical strategies, because wisdom matters. Recognizing vulnerable times, restructuring environments, and inviting trusted accountability are all necessary steps. But they will be framed properly. Boundaries are not punishment. Accountability is not surveillance. Both exist to protect alignment and foster healing without guilt or shame.

You were never meant to fight alone. Isolation feeds addiction. Light weakens it. When struggles are shared in a safe, mature community, their power diminishes. Healing accelerates when shame loses its secrecy.

If you are reading this, you are not alone, and you are not beyond hope. Your struggle does not disqualify you from God's presence. It reveals your need for it. Freedom is not the absence of temptation. It is the restored alignment that trains desire toward what is life-giving.

This journey will require honesty, patience, and grace. It will also require courage. But freedom is worth the process.

Healing is possible. Identity can be restored. Intimacy can be renewed.

This book is an invitation to step into the light, not with fear, but with trust. God is already present there.

Chapter 1 The Addiction No One Talks About

"For anything that becomes visible is light."
(Ephesians 5:13, ESV)

Core Truth: Silence empowers bondage.

A Battle Hidden Behind Strength

During my years of military service, I learned that not every battle is fought in visible terrain. Some battles are carried quietly by disciplined men and women who function well under pressure, lead effectively, and appear strong to everyone around them. The most dangerous battles were often the ones no one spoke about, because silence isolates, and isolation weakens resolve.

That lesson followed me into ministry.

In churches, counseling rooms, and private conversations, I began to see a pattern. Faithful believers, leaders, spouses, and young adults were wrestling with something they felt deeply ashamed to name. They prayed sincerely. They served faithfully. Yet behind closed doors, many were fighting a struggle they did not know how to bring into the light.

Pornography was rarely mentioned openly, but it was frequently present.

This was not a problem of weak faith or moral apathy. It was a problem of secrecy.

Pornography does not announce itself loudly. It embeds itself quietly, often beginning long before someone understands its weight. It hides behind privacy, late hours, stress, loneliness, boredom, or curiosity. Because it is hidden, it becomes isolated. Because it is isolated, it grows stronger.

Silence does not make sin disappear. It gives it room to deepen.

A Hidden Struggle Across Demographics

One of the most damaging misconceptions about pornography is the belief that it affects only a narrow group of people. It is often framed as a men's issue, a youth issue, or a lack-of-discipline issue. In reality, pornography does not discriminate.

It affects men and women.
It affects the married and unmarried.
It affects leaders and new believers.
It affects the disciplined and the struggling alike.

Technology has erased many of the barriers that once limited exposure. What once required deliberate effort is now passively accessible. Phones and devices are personal, private, and constant. Exposure often happens early, sometimes unintentionally, long before maturity or discernment has been formed. What begins as curiosity can become a habit. What becomes habit can shape desire.

Many people do not stumble into pornography because they are rebellious. They stumble because they are human, formed in a digital environment that offers instant gratification without relationship, effort, or accountability.

The hidden nature of pornography allows people to function outwardly while slowly fragmenting inwardly. This fragmentation produces confusion. A person can love God sincerely and still feel trapped. They can desire holiness and still feel powerless. When this contradiction remains unaddressed, shame grows.

Why Secrecy Strengthens the Bondage

Pornography thrives in secrecy because secrecy removes resistance. When a struggle is hidden, it is no longer challenged by truth, community, or light. The mind begins to compartmentalize. Behavior is separated from identity. Faith becomes something practiced publicly while pain is managed privately.

Shame plays a critical role here. Shame does not say, "You did something wrong." Shame says, "You are something wrong." Once shame takes root, people stop seeking help and start hiding patterns. They avoid conversation. They avoid prayer that feels honest. They avoid accountability that feels risky.

This mirrors a pattern established early in Scripture. When Adam and Eve sinned, they did not run toward God for restoration. They hid. Not because God could not see them, but because shame altered their posture. Hiding changed their awareness of His presence.

Pornography produces a similar posture. The more someone hides, the less aware they become of God's nearness, not because God has withdrawn, but because shame has distorted perception. Over time, this dulls spiritual sensitivity and creates distance in experience, even when the relationship still exists.

Secrecy does not protect people from judgment. It protects bondage from exposure.

When Discipleship Remains Silent

Many assume the reason pornography remains hidden is that people are unwilling to speak. In many cases, the opposite is true. People want help. They want guidance. They want freedom. What they often encounter instead is silence or shallow correction.

Pornography has frequently been addressed only indirectly or avoided altogether in discipleship. Sometimes leaders fear being too explicit. Sometimes they feel unprepared. Sometimes they assume someone else will address it. The result is the same. Where discipleship remains silent, people fill the gap with shame and self-effort.

This is not a failure of believers. It is often a failure of formation.

When the church does not provide language, context, and pathways for healing, individuals attempt to navigate complex struggles alone. They rely on willpower, guilt, or promises to change. These tools fail not because people do not care, but because transformation does not occur through pressure alone.

Discipleship was never meant to be silent about struggles that shape identity, intimacy, and formation. Silence does not preserve purity. It preserves confusion.

Silence Is Not Neutral

Silence always communicates something. When pornography is ignored, minimized, or avoided, the unspoken message is often interpreted as disqualification or hopelessness. People assume that if the church is not addressing it, their struggle must be beyond grace or too shameful to mention.

This belief keeps people trapped longer than the behavior itself.

The purpose of addressing pornography is not exposure for exposure's sake. It is restoration. Light does not exist to humiliate. It exists to heal. Naming the struggle does not increase its power. It weakens it.

This chapter exists to say clearly what many need to hear. You are not alone. Your struggle is not unique. Your desire for freedom is valid. And silence is not your ally.

Breaking bondage begins when secrecy ends. Freedom starts when the light is allowed in. The chapters ahead will move deeper into understanding what pornography does, why it has such power, and how healing unfolds. But it begins here, by naming what has too often remained unspoken.

Silence empowers bondage.
Truth, spoken with grace, breaks it.

Reflection

1. What makes this struggle difficult to speak about honestly?
2. Where has silence shaped how you view yourself or your faith?
3. Have you ever equated secrecy with protection? What has it actually produced?
4. In what ways might shame have altered your awareness of God's presence?
5. What would it look like to step into the light without fear of condemnation?

Chapter 2 How We Got Here

*"Do not be conformed to this world, but be transformed by
the renewal of your mind."*
(Romans 12:2, ESV)

Core Truth: Technology is neutral; formation is not.

Technology Is a Tool, Not a Villain

It is tempting to place the blame for pornography squarely on
technology. Phones, tablets, laptops, and high-speed internet
have certainly changed the landscape. Yet technology itself is
not the root problem. Tools do not possess moral agency.
They amplify what already exists in the human heart.

Throughout this book, the word *formative* is used
intentionally. Something is formative not because it is
dramatic or obvious, but because it quietly shapes how we
think, desire, and respond over time. Formation happens
through repetition, exposure, and attention, often without
awareness. What forms us eventually directs us.

Technology has brought extraordinary benefits. It connects
families across distance. It provides education, efficiency, and
access to information that previous generations could not

imagine. Like any powerful tool, however, it shapes formation when used without intention.

The issue is not that technology exists. The issue is that it forms habits, desires, and reflexes faster than most people realize. When formation is unintentional, desire is shaped by exposure rather than wisdom. Technology becomes the environment in which the mind is trained, often without awareness.

Pornography did not begin with the internet, but the internet removed friction. What once required effort, risk, and visibility now requires nothing more than privacy and curiosity. When effort is removed, restraint weakens. When restraint weakens, repetition increases. Over time, repetition forms an appetite.

Technology did not create desire. It trained it.

Accessibility and Anonymity

Two features of modern technology have significantly accelerated the spread of pornography: accessibility and anonymity.

Accessibility means pornography is always close. Devices are carried constantly, often within arm's reach from morning until night. Moments of stress, boredom, loneliness, or fatigue are now immediately paired with opportunity. There is little time between impulse and access.

Anonymity compounds this problem. Consumption happens privately, without witnesses, without accountability, and often without immediate consequence. This privacy creates the illusion that behavior exists in isolation. The mind begins to separate what is done in secret from who a person believes themselves to be in public.

Anonymity reduces internal resistance. It removes social restraint, moral interruption, and communal awareness. Over time, secrecy becomes a habit, not just of behavior, but of thought. This pattern trains the mind to associate desire with isolation rather than relationship.

What is repeated in secrecy gains strength without challenge.

The Myth of Age Verification

Most pornographic sites display some form of age verification, usually a simple confirmation asking if the viewer is over a certain age. In practice, these prompts function more as disclaimers than barriers.

Children and adolescents are not protected by these systems. Early exposure is often accidental, unintentional, or curiosity-driven. A search, a link, a shared device, or peer exposure can open a door long before maturity, discernment, or emotional readiness is present.

Early exposure matters because the brain is still forming. The developing mind does not interpret content the same way an adult mind does. Images encountered early do not remain neutral memories. They become reference points. They influence expectation, curiosity, and future desire.

Early Exposure and Neurological Imprinting

The brain is designed to learn through repetition and reward. When a stimulus produces pleasure, the brain remembers it. Dopamine reinforces pathways associated with that experience, encouraging repetition.

When exposure to pornography occurs early, especially during developmental years, it can imprint patterns before relational maturity has developed. The brain begins to associate arousal with images rather than connection, novelty rather than intimacy, consumption rather than participation.

This imprinting does not doom a person. It explains why later change can feel difficult. Neural pathways strengthened over time do not disappear instantly. They must be reshaped through new patterns, new attention, and renewed formation.

Understanding this is important because it removes moral confusion. Struggle does not automatically mean desire for sin. Often, it reflects learned pathways that were never consciously chosen.

Formation happened before understanding. Healing requires intentional reformation.

A Brief Look at the Landscape

The goal of statistics is not to overwhelm or alarm, but to establish awareness. Pornography is not a fringe issue. It is a cultural reality.

A significant majority of internet users will encounter pornography at some point in their lives.

The average age of first exposure is often reported in early adolescence, with many encountering explicit material before their teenage years.

Usage spans genders, with men historically consuming at higher rates, but with female usage steadily increasing. Frequency trends show that for many, consumption is not occasional, but habitual, often tied to stress, fatigue, or emotional regulation.

These numbers simply confirm what many already sense privately. This struggle is widespread.

Normalization does not make something healthy. But understanding its prevalence helps dismantle the lie of isolation.

Formation Happens Whether We Choose It or Not

Every environment forms something. The question is not whether formation is happening, but what is doing the forming.

When technology fills unguarded space, it trains attention. When content is consumed without reflection, it shapes imagination. When habits develop without accountability, they become patterns of thought and desire.

Technology is not evil. But unexamined exposure is powerful.

This chapter is not about assigning blame. It is about naming reality. We did not arrive here because people suddenly lost morality. We arrived here because formation accelerated while discipleship often lagged behind.

Freedom begins with understanding. Change begins when formation becomes intentional. The chapters ahead will explore what pornography does to the mind, the body, and the spirit. But before healing can occur, it helps to understand how we got here.

Reflection

1. How has technology shaped your habits more than you may have realized?
2. When did exposure to explicit content first occur, and how might that timing have influenced formation?
3. In what ways has anonymity made certain behaviors easier to repeat?
4. How does understanding neurological formation change the way you view struggle?
5. What areas of formation in your life have been unintentional rather than deliberate?

Chapter 3 The Psychological Impact

"All things are lawful for me ... but I will not be dominated by anything."
(1 Corinthians 6:12, ESV)

Core Truth: Repetition reshapes desire.

The Brain Was Designed to Learn This Way

The human brain is remarkably efficient. It is designed to learn from experience, reinforce what feels rewarding, and repeat what appears beneficial. This design is not flawed. It is purposeful. God created the brain to associate pleasure with life-giving activities such as connection, bonding, creativity, and rest.

When something produces pleasure, the brain releases chemicals that reinforce the experience. Dopamine plays a central role in motivation and anticipation, while endorphins contribute to sensations of pleasure and relief. Together, they help the brain remember what felt good and encourage repetition.

This system is essential for survival and healthy attachment. It motivates learning, perseverance, and relational bonding.

However, like any system, it can be trained toward unhealthy patterns when repeatedly paired with stimuli that were never meant to carry that weight.

Pornography hijacks a system designed for connection and redirects it toward consumption.

Dopamine, Endorphins, and the Training of Desire

Dopamine is often misunderstood as a pleasure chemical alone. In reality, dopamine is closely tied to motivation and anticipation. It increases when the brain expects a reward, not just when the reward is received. This anticipation drives pursuit.

Pornography stimulates dopamine by offering novelty, accessibility, and immediate gratification. Each new image, category, or experience signals potential reward. The brain learns to anticipate pleasure quickly and repeatedly.

Endorphins reinforce the experience by providing a sense of release or relief. For some, this relief is emotional rather than physical, temporarily reducing stress, anxiety, or loneliness. Over time, the brain begins to associate pornography not only with pleasure, but with regulation. It becomes a coping mechanism.

This matters because the brain does not distinguish between healthy and unhealthy sources of relief. It only recognizes patterns. What is repeated becomes familiar. What is familiar becomes preferred.

Desire is not merely chosen. It is trained.

The Reward System and Habit Formation

The brain's reward system strengthens pathways that are used frequently. Each repetition reinforces neural connections, making them easier to activate in the future. This is why habits form. It is also why habits feel automatic over time.

With pornography, repetition can shift desire from relational engagement to solitary consumption. The brain learns to associate arousal with speed, novelty, and control rather than patience, presence, and mutuality. This does not mean someone no longer values real intimacy. It means the brain has been trained to expect a different pattern of stimulation.

Eventually, the reward system adapts. What once produced a strong response becomes less effective. The brain seeks greater stimulation to achieve the same level of reward. This is known as desensitization.

Desensitization is not a moral failure. It is a neurological adaptation.

Desensitization and the Pull Toward Escalation

As desensitization occurs, the brain requires increased novelty or intensity to produce the same response. This is why content often escalates over time. What once felt shocking may eventually feel ordinary. What once felt sufficient may feel dull.

Escalation does not always mean more extreme content. Sometimes it means more time, more frequency, or more isolation. Sometimes it involves shifting preferences or reduced satisfaction with real relationships.

This pattern creates confusion. People often ask why something they once resisted now feels harder to avoid. The answer is not that desire has grown stronger. It is that sensitivity has diminished.

Understanding this removes unnecessary shame. Escalation is a predictable outcome of repeated stimulation, not evidence of deeper moral corruption. That does not excuse behavior, but it does explain the struggle.

Healing requires retraining sensitivity, not just suppressing impulse.

Why Novelty Becomes Addictive

The human brain is wired to notice novelty. Newness captures attention because it may signal opportunity or threat. In healthy contexts, novelty fuels curiosity, creativity, and learning.

Pornography exploits this wiring by offering endless novelty without effort or risk. The brain receives repeated dopamine spikes from new stimuli, reinforcing the pursuit of variety rather than depth. Over time, novelty becomes the primary driver of desire.

This is why scrolling can feel compulsive. The next image always holds potential reward. Anticipation becomes addictive, even when satisfaction decreases.

Novelty trains impatience. It reduces tolerance for slow, ordinary, relational experiences. This does not mean real intimacy loses its value. It means the brain has been conditioned to expect constant stimulation.
Formation has taken place.

From Behavior to Formation

At this point, it becomes clear why pornography cannot be addressed as a simple behavior problem. Behavior is the surface expression of deeper patterns. The brain has been trained through repetition, reward, and reinforcement.

This training did not happen overnight, and it cannot be undone through willpower alone. Telling someone to stop without addressing the formation is like asking a retrained muscle to perform without rehabilitation. Effort alone leads to frustration.

The encouraging truth is that the brain is adaptable. Neural pathways can be reshaped. Sensitivity can be restored. Desire can be retrained. But this requires intentional formation, patience, and alignment.

This chapter marks a shift. The conversation is no longer about what people do, but about how they have been formed. Understanding this prepares the way for compassion, wisdom, and sustainable change.

The chapters ahead will explore how these psychological patterns intersect with the body and the spirit, and how restoration becomes possible when formation is addressed at its root.

Reflection

1. How does understanding the brain's reward system change the way you view desire?
2. In what ways might repetition have shaped habits without conscious choice?
3. Have you noticed patterns of desensitization or diminished satisfaction over time?
4. How has novelty influenced attention, patience, or expectations?
5. What does it mean to consider healing as retraining rather than punishment?

Chapter 4 The Physical and Relational Cost

*"So God created man in his own image, in
the image of God he created him; male
and female he created them."*
(Genesis 1:27, ESV)

Core Truth: What trains the mind weakens intimacy.

When Expectations Are Quietly Rewritten

Pornography does not simply show images. Over time, it teaches expectations. Without ever announcing itself as instruction, it presents a version of intimacy that is scripted, edited, and disconnected from a real relationship. The mind absorbs these patterns gradually, often without awareness.

Real intimacy is mutual, imperfect, and relational. It involves communication, vulnerability, patience, and responsiveness to another person. Pornography, by contrast, centers the viewer. It removes the need to respond, to adapt, or to consider another's experience. Over time, this contrast matters.

When expectations are shaped by fantasy rather than a relationship, disappointment can follow. Real people cannot compete with curated images. Real intimacy unfolds slowly, while pornography offers instant stimulation. This gap can create frustration, confusion, or dissatisfaction, not because real intimacy lacks value, but because the mind has been trained to expect something different.

This training does not mean that the desire for a real connection disappears. It means desire has been misdirected.

Performance Anxiety and the Weight of Comparison

One of the quieter costs of pornography is performance anxiety. When arousal is conditioned to highly stimulating, novel, or unrealistic scenarios, the body may struggle to respond in ordinary relational contexts. This can be deeply discouraging, especially for those who desire healthy intimacy.

Some experience difficulty maintaining arousal. Others feel pressure to perform or fear disappointment. These experiences can feel personal, even shameful, yet they often reflect conditioning rather than deficiency.

The body responds to what it has been trained to expect. When expectations are unrealistic, anxiety follows. Anxiety disrupts presence. Presence is essential for intimacy.

It is important to say clearly that these struggles are not permanent. The body is responsive. Sensitivity can be restored. The same adaptability that allowed conditioning also allows healing. Understanding this replaces fear with patience.

When Desire for Real Intimacy Diminishes

Many people feel unsettled when they notice reduced desire for real intimacy. They may still love their spouse or long for a relationship, yet feel disconnected or uninterested. This can create guilt, confusion, or self-judgment.

Pornography conditions the brain toward ease and control. Real intimacy requires engagement, responsiveness, and emotional availability. When the mind has been trained toward quick release without effort, relational desire can feel demanding by comparison.

This does not mean real intimacy has lost its worth. It means effort now feels unfamiliar. Desire has been redirected, not erased.

The encouraging truth is that desire follows attention. What is consistently attended to grows in influence. When attention is redirected toward presence, connection, and relationship, desire can be retrained.

Ease Over Effort

Pornography offers intimacy without effort. There is no need to communicate, reconcile, serve, or persevere. This convenience subtly trains the heart to avoid the work that real intimacy requires.

Over time, this preference for ease can extend beyond sexuality. Emotional withdrawal, avoidance of conflict, and reduced patience can follow. When effort feels burdensome, relationships suffer.

Real intimacy is costly, but it is also deeply rewarding. It builds trust, safety, and shared meaning. It matures desire rather than exhausting it.

Effort is not the enemy of intimacy. It is the pathway to depth.

Hope for Restoration

It is important to pause here and speak clearly. The physical and relational effects of pornography are real, but they are

not final. The brain can heal. The body can respond.
Relationships can be restored.

Healing does not happen through pressure or panic. It
happens through patience, understanding, and intentional
realignment. When pornography is removed as the primary
source of stimulation, sensitivity gradually returns. When
presence replaces consumption, intimacy regains its strength.

This process takes time. That does not mean it is failing. It
means it is working.

The goal is not perfection. The goal is reconnection. Intimacy
was designed to be shared, not consumed. It thrives where
trust, presence, and patience are cultivated.

What has been trained can be retrained. What has been
weakened can be strengthened. Hope remains because
formation is not fixed.

Reflection

1. In what ways might expectations have been shaped without your awareness?
2. How has anxiety or comparison affected intimacy or connection?
3. Have you noticed a preference for ease over effort in relationships?
4. What fears surface when thinking about restoration or change?
5. How does knowing that retraining is possible reshape your sense of hope?

Chapter 5 The Spiritual Consequences of Hiding

"Where shall I go from your Spirit? Or where
shall I flee from your presence?"
(Psalm 139:7, ESV)

Core Truth: God does not leave us; we withdraw from awareness.

Gratification Without Covenant

Pornography offers something that appears intimate but carries no commitment. It provides stimulation without responsibility, pleasure without presence, and release without relationship. This is why it is so spiritually disruptive. It trains the heart to receive without giving and to experience without covenant.

Covenant is not merely a rule. It is the context in which intimacy becomes meaningful. Covenant requires trust, patience, mutuality, and faithfulness. It invites two people into shared vulnerability and responsibility. Pornography removes that context entirely.

Instant gratification feels powerful because it bypasses waiting. It promises satisfaction now, without the work of a relationship or the risk of rejection. Over time, this trains the soul to prefer immediacy over faithfulness. Desire becomes impatient. Connection becomes optional.

Spiritually, this matters because God's design for intimacy has always been covenantal. From the beginning, intimacy was meant to reflect a relationship, not consumption. When gratification is separated from covenant, intimacy is hollowed out, and the soul learns a pattern that does not translate into life-giving connection.

False Intimacy Versus True Connection

Pornography presents a convincing imitation of intimacy. Images appear personal. Scenarios feel relational. Yet nothing is shared, and nothing is received in return. The viewer remains unseen and unchanged by the encounter.

True intimacy involves being known. It requires presence, honesty, and mutual awareness. It is shaped by communication and sustained through trust. Pornography offers none of these. It offers stimulation without vulnerability and fantasy without commitment.

This false intimacy not only affects relationships with others. It subtly reshapes how a person approaches God. When intimacy is practiced as consumption, prayer can become transactional. Worship can become distant. Scripture can feel flat. The heart becomes accustomed to engagement without surrender.

Over time, this pattern dulls spiritual sensitivity. Not because God has withdrawn, but because the soul has been trained to seek connection without presence.

The First Pattern of Hiding

Scripture offers an early and revealing picture of what happens when shame enters the human experience. After Adam and Eve sinned, their immediate response was not rebellion or denial. It was hiding.

They hid from God, not because He was no longer present, but because shame altered their posture. They covered themselves. They avoided exposure. They attempted to manage their condition privately.

God's response is instructive. He did not leave the garden. He did not abandon them. He came looking, asking a question that revealed a relationship rather than distance. Where are you?
This question was not about location. It was about awareness.

Pornography creates a similar pattern. Shame encourages hiding. Hiding creates distance in experience. Over time, people begin to believe God feels far away. They assume intimacy with Him has been compromised. In reality, awareness has been dulled.

The pattern is ancient. The struggle is modern. The solution remains the same. God seeks His people even when they hide.

Shame and the Dulling of Awareness

Shame is not the same as conviction. Conviction draws a person toward God with honesty and hope. Shame drives a person inward, toward isolation and self-protection.

When shame becomes dominant, spiritual practices often change subtly. Prayer becomes guarded. Confession becomes vague. Worship becomes performative. Scripture becomes something to analyze rather than encounter.

This does not happen because God has changed. It happens because shame reshapes perception. The heart becomes hesitant. Awareness becomes muted. The presence of God feels distant, even when it remains constant.

Pornography thrives in this environment. When shame dulls awareness of God's nearness, temptation feels stronger, and resistance feels weaker. The struggle becomes cyclical. Shame leads to hiding. Hiding leads to numbness. Numbness leads to more seeking of false relief.

This cycle is not broken through self-condemnation. It is broken through restored awareness.

God's Nearness Has Not Changed

It is essential to say this plainly.

The danger is not that God withdraws.
The danger is that hiding makes us unaware of Him.

God does not abandon His children in struggle. Scripture consistently reveals a God who draws near to the broken, the tempted, and the weary. He is not repelled by weakness. He is moved by honesty.

When someone feels distant from God, the answer is not more effort or louder promises. It is gentler honesty. It is bringing what has been hidden into the light of His presence.

Awareness returns where hiding ends.

Stepping Back Into the Light

The path forward is not dramatic. It is humble. It begins by acknowledging reality without excuses or despair. It involves naming what has been hidden and allowing God's presence to meet it.

This is not about confessing perfectly or resolving everything at once. It is about posture. Turning toward God rather than away. Allowing His nearness to become felt again.

As awareness is restored, shame loses its power. Desire begins to realign. Temptation does not vanish, but it no longer operates in isolation. Light changes the environment.

The chapters ahead will address repentance, renewal of the mind, and practical pathways toward freedom. But those steps are effective only when this foundation is laid. God is not distant. He is present. Healing begins when we stop hiding from that reality.

Reflection

1. In what ways might instant gratification have replaced covenantal connection?
2. How have patterns of hiding shaped your awareness of God's presence?
3. What is the difference between conviction and shame in your experience?
4. Where have you assumed distance from God rather than dulled awareness?
5. What would it look like to step into the light with honesty rather than fear?

Chapter 6 Behavior Is Not the Root

*"Keep your heart with all vigilance, for
from it flow the springs of life."*
(Proverbs 4:23, ESV)

Core Truth: Spiritual disorder produces behavioral cycles.

Why Behavior-Focused Solutions Fail

When people want freedom from pornography, the first
instinct is often to focus on stopping the behavior. Delete the
app. Make a rule. Try harder. Promise God it will never
happen again. These efforts are usually sincere, and they
often work for a short time.

But short-term success frequently gives way to long-term
frustration.

Behavior-focused solutions fail not because discipline is
unimportant, but because discipline alone cannot heal what it
did not create. Behavior is the visible expression of something
deeper. When the deeper issue remains untouched, behavior
eventually returns, often with greater force and increased
shame.

This cycle is exhausting. Each failure reinforces the belief that something is fundamentally wrong with the person rather than with the approach. Over time, people stop believing freedom is possible and settle for management instead of healing.

Stopping behavior without addressing formation is like treating pain without addressing injury. Relief may come temporarily, but restoration does not.

Symptoms Versus Formation

Pornography is a symptom. It expresses deeper realities related to desire, identity, coping, and connection. When stress, loneliness, boredom, or emotional fatigue surface, learned patterns activate automatically. The behavior provides familiarity and temporary relief.

Treating symptoms alone creates a cycle of suppression and release. Suppression increases pressure. Pressure seeks escape. Escape reinforces the habit. The cycle repeats.

Formation works differently. Formation addresses how the heart has been trained to seek comfort, relief, and meaning. It examines where desire has been shaped and how attention has been directed over time. When formation changes, behavior follows naturally.

This is why lasting change often feels slower at first but more stable over time. Formation does not aim for immediate compliance. It aims for realignment.

Healing formation takes patience. But it produces freedom rather than fear.

The Heart Before the Habit

Scripture consistently points to the heart as the source of action. Not the heart as emotion alone, but the heart as the center of desire, attention, and allegiance. What the heart trusts, the life follows.

When pornography becomes a go-to response, it often reveals unmet needs or misdirected desire. It may be used to regulate emotion, escape pressure, or seek affirmation. These needs are not sinful. They are human. The issue lies in where they are taken for fulfillment.

Addressing the heart does not excuse behavior. It explains it. Explanation allows healing without shame.

Habits are not broken by condemnation. They are replaced by deeper satisfaction. When the heart learns to turn toward God for comfort, truth, and presence, the habit loses its role.

This is why transformation begins internally. Change becomes sustainable when desire is retrained rather than merely restrained.

The Way Jesus Transformed People

Jesus rarely began with behavior correction. He began with an invitation.

When He encountered people trapped in cycles of sin, shame, or dysfunction, He did not reduce them to their behavior. He saw the person first. He restored dignity before demanding change. He addressed identity before instruction.

Transformation in the ministry of Jesus flowed from a relationship. He invited people to follow Him, to be with Him, to learn a new way of seeing God, themselves, and the world. Behavior changed as alignment deepened.

This does not mean Jesus ignored sin. It means He addressed it at the right level. He dealt with the heart so that obedience could become an expression of love rather than fear.

Freedom followed proximity.

This model matters because it shows that transformation is relational before it is behavioral. The goal is not control, but communion.

From Control to Alignment

Many people attempt to overcome pornography by exerting more control. Control focuses on managing impulses. Alignment focuses on reordering desire.

Control asks, How do I stop this?
Alignment asks, What is my heart seeking?

When alignment is restored, control becomes less necessary. Temptation does not vanish, but it loses authority. Desire becomes integrated rather than fragmented.

This chapter marks a shift. The goal is no longer simply to stop a behavior. The goal is to restore spiritual order. When God is returned to the center of desire, behavior reorganizes naturally around that reality.

The chapters ahead will explore repentance, renewal of the mind, boundaries, and accountability. These are not tools for self-control. They are pathways for alignment.

Behavior is not the root; formation is.

Reflection

1. What behavior-focused strategies have you relied on in the past?
2. How have cycles of suppression and relapse shaped your expectations?
3. What needs or desires might be operating beneath the habit?
4. How does shifting from control to alignment change your view of freedom?
5. What would it look like to pursue transformation rather than management?

Chapter 7 Repentance That Transforms

*"Create in me a clean heart, O God, and
renew a right spirit within me."*
(Psalm 51:10, ESV)

Core Truth: Repentance is alignment, not self-punishment.

Repentance as Scripture Describes It

Repentance is one of the most misunderstood words in the
Christian life. Many associate it with shame, regret, or
emotional self-condemnation. Others reduce it to saying
sorry or making promises to do better. Scripture presents
something far richer and far more hopeful.

Biblical repentance is a change of mind that results in a
change of direction. It is not merely sorrow over behavior,
but a realignment of thinking, desire, and trust. Repentance
does not begin with self-hatred. It begins with truth.

True repentance turns a person toward God, not inward
toward punishment. It acknowledges reality honestly and
then responds by reordering life around what is true. This is
why repentance produces freedom rather than despair.

Punishment-based repentance focuses on failure. Transformative repentance focuses on alignment.

Why Willpower Alone Fails

Many people attempt repentance through willpower. They grit their teeth, set rules, and rely on discipline to overpower desire. While discipline has value, it cannot carry the weight of transformation on its own.

Willpower operates at the level of behavior. It attempts to restrain desire without reshaping it. Over time, restraint becomes exhausting. Desire eventually seeks release, often with greater intensity.

This is not because people lack sincerity. It is because desire has not been addressed. The heart continues to want what it has been trained to want. Willpower can delay behavior, but it cannot heal formation.

Lasting repentance requires something deeper than effort. It requires renewal.

Asking the Holy Spirit to Renew Desire

Transformation begins when the work shifts from self-management to surrender. Scripture teaches that renewal is the work of the Spirit, not the product of human striving. The

Holy Spirit does not merely help us resist sin. He reshapes desire itself.

This begins with honest prayer. Not rehearsed promises or dramatic vows, but simple truth. Naming what has been desired. Naming what has been sought for comfort, relief, or escape. Then, inviting God to re-train the heart.

Renewal does not mean temptation disappears overnight. It means desire begins to loosen its grip. What once felt necessary begins to feel optional. What once demanded attention begins to lose authority.

This process takes time. That does not mean repentance has failed. It means formation is changing.

Repentance that transforms is patient because it trusts God's work more than personal effort.

Learning to See Clearly Again

One of the quiet effects of pornography is distorted vision. People become images. Bodies become objects. Desire becomes detached from dignity. This distortion does not happen because people stop valuing others. It happens because repetition trains perception.
Repentance involves learning to see again.

To see that the person on a screen is not content to be consumed. They are someone's son or daughter. They have a history, a story, a family, and a soul. They are created in the image of God.

This shift matters deeply. Desire loses power when perception changes. When people are no longer reduced to objects, consumption loses its justification. Respect reenters the heart. Compassion interrupts impulse.

This is not about shaming past behavior. It is about restoring vision.

People are not content.
They are God's sons and daughters.

Alignment Produces Fruit

Repentance that transforms does not end in guilt. It produces fruit. As alignment deepens, behavior begins to change naturally. Not because rules are tighter, but because desire is different.

This is how Scripture consistently describes transformation. Old patterns lose relevance as new ones take their place. The heart turns toward what gives life rather than what numbs it.

Alignment does not make a person flawless. It makes them honest, dependent, and aware. When failure occurs, it no longer leads to hiding. It leads back to God.

This is the difference between punishment and repentance. One drives people away. The other draws them closer.

From Shame to Surrender

Shame says, You must punish yourself before you can approach God.
Repentance says, Come to God so that you can be restored.

When repentance is understood rightly, fear loses its grip. Honesty becomes possible. Desire becomes trainable. Freedom becomes realistic.

This chapter marks a turning point. You are no longer stuck trying harder. You are learning to surrender more deeply. What follows will build on this foundation with practical wisdom, renewed thinking, and supportive structures.

Repentance is not about proving sincerity.
It is about returning to alignment.

Alignment restores what effort never could. As you turn toward God rather than striving to manage yourself, transformation becomes a process of trust, not punishment.

Reflection

1. How have you previously understood repentance?
2. Where have you relied on willpower rather than renewal?
3. What desires might need to be reshaped rather than suppressed?
4. How does seeing people as image-bearers change the way you think about consumption?
5. What would surrender look like in this season rather than punishment?

Chapter 8 Renewing the Mind

"We all, with unveiled face, beholding the glory of the Lord, are being transformed into the same image."
(2 Corinthians 3:18, ESV)

Core Truth: What you behold trains what you desire.

Renewal Is Both Spiritual and Practical

Renewal of the mind is often spoken of in spiritual language, but it is also deeply practical. The mind is not renewed through passive intention. It is renewed through attention. What the mind repeatedly attends, shapes what the heart begins to want.

This is why Scripture places such emphasis on thought life. Renewal does not require perfection. It requires redirection. Each moment of attention becomes a formative moment.

Pornography trains the mind through repeated exposure. Renewal trains the mind through repeated presence. Both rely on the same principle. Repetition reshapes pathways. The difference lies in what is being repeated.

Renewal is not about erasing the past. It is about forming a new future through intentional beholding.

Prayer as Neurological and Spiritual Renewal

Prayer is often understood as communication with God. It is also participation in transformation. When prayer becomes habitual, it reshapes attention, emotion, and awareness.

In moments of temptation, prayer interrupts automatic patterns. It creates a pause. That pause allows the brain to shift from impulse to awareness. Over time, repeated pauses weaken old pathways and strengthen new ones.

Prayer does not need to be long or elaborate. Simple, honest prayer realigns focus. It reorients desire toward presence rather than escape. As prayer becomes a first response rather than a last resort, the mind learns a new association.

Prayer trains the brain to seek relief through connection rather than consumption.

Scripture as Re-Patterning Truth

Scripture functions as more than information. It provides truth that re-patterns thoughts. When Scripture is read slowly, reflectively, and repeatedly, it reshapes how reality is interpreted.

Pornography distorts perception by normalizing consumption and detachment. Scripture restores perspective by revealing dignity, purpose, and truth. Over time, these truths replace distorted narratives.

This does not require memorizing large portions immediately. It requires consistency. One verse repeated can reshape thoughts more effectively than many verses read without reflection.

Truth re-patterns what repetition has distorted.

Interrupting Thought Cycles

Thoughts often move in predictable cycles. A trigger appears. Attention follows. Desire intensifies. Behavior feels inevitable. Interrupting this cycle requires awareness rather than force.

Awareness notices the thought without agreeing with it. It names the moment. This moment of naming creates space. Within that space, choice becomes possible.

Interrupting a thought cycle does not mean suppressing thoughts. Suppression often increases their power. Instead, interruption redirects attention. Prayer, Scripture, movement, or conversation can all serve as redirection tools.

Over time, repeated interruptions weaken the cycle. The brain learns new patterns. Desire becomes less automatic.

Renewal happens one interruption at a time.

Replacing Consumption With Communion

Freedom is not sustained by avoidance alone. Something must replace what is removed. Pornography often fills a space of loneliness, stress, or fatigue. If that space remains empty, old habits return.

Communion addresses the underlying need. Communion is relational presence. It includes time with God, connection with others, and engagement with life-giving practices.

This replacement is not symbolic. It is practical. Time spent in prayer, conversation, creativity, or rest retrains the mind toward fullness rather than escape.

Consumption isolates. Communion connects.

As communion becomes habitual, desire shifts. What once felt necessary becomes less compelling. The heart learns to seek life where it is found.

Formation Through Attention

Renewing the mind is not a single decision. It is a daily practice. Each moment of attention becomes a moment of formation. This does not require perfection. It requires persistence.

What you behold repeatedly will shape what you desire eventually. The mind learns through exposure. Renewal simply changes what is being exposed.

This chapter marks a shift from understanding to practice. The chapters ahead will focus on boundaries, accountability, and walking in the light. These practices support renewal by protecting attention and reinforcing formation.

Renewal is not about trying harder.
It is about beholding differently.

Reflection

1. What currently captures most of your attention during moments of stress or fatigue?
2. How might prayer function as an interruption rather than an obligation?
3. What Scriptures could be returned to repeatedly for re-patterning truth?
4. What thought cycles tend to lead toward old habits?
5. What practices of communion could replace patterns of consumption?

Chapter 9 Boundaries That Protect, Not Punish

"Ponder the path of your feet; then all
your ways will be sure.
Do not swerve to the right or to the left; turn
your foot away from evil."
(Proverbs 4:26-27, ESV)

Core Truth: Boundaries create space for freedom.

Boundaries Are an Act of Wisdom

Boundaries are often misunderstood as restrictions meant to control behavior. In reality, boundaries exist to protect what matters most. They are not expressions of fear or weakness. They are expressions of clarity.

When boundaries are framed as punishment, people resist them. When they are understood as protection, people embrace them. Healthy boundaries acknowledge human limitations without condemning them. They create space where freedom can grow.

Pornography thrives where access is easy and awareness is low. Boundaries interrupt this environment by reducing opportunity and increasing intentionality. They do not replace the renewal of the mind. They support it.

Freedom flourishes where wisdom is practiced consistently.

Recognizing Vulnerable Times

Most lapses do not occur randomly. They follow patterns. At certain times of day, emotional states, or circumstances increase vulnerability. Fatigue, stress, loneliness, boredom, and emotional overload often lower resistance.

Recognizing vulnerability is not an admission of weakness. It is an act of awareness. Awareness allows preparation. Preparation reduces surprise.

Many people notice increased temptation late at night, during periods of isolation, or after emotionally demanding days. Identifying these windows allows boundaries to be placed proactively rather than reactively.

Boundaries work best when they anticipate reality rather than denying it.

Environmental Awareness

Environment shapes behavior more than intention alone. What is accessible, visible, and convenient influences choice.

Awareness of the environment allows it to be structured wisely.

This includes physical space, digital space, and social space. Private environments with unrestricted access invite secrecy. Shared environments with visibility encourage accountability.

Environmental awareness does not mean living in fear. It means choosing settings that support alignment. Small changes in the environment can significantly reduce pressure.

The environment is a silent teacher. Boundaries decide what it teaches.

Strategic Resistance

Resistance is most effective when it is planned rather than improvised. Strategic resistance acknowledges that temptation will arise and prepares responses ahead of time.

This may involve predetermined actions when urges surface. Standing up, changing location, initiating conversation, or engaging in physical movement can interrupt an impulse. These actions redirect attention and allow renewed choices.

Strategic resistance does not rely on emotion. It relies on preparation. When resistance is practiced consistently, it becomes familiar rather than exhausting.

Preparation turns moments of temptation into moments of decision rather than defeat.

Immediate Prayer as Reorientation

When urges surface, immediate prayer functions as reorientation rather than an emergency response. It does not need to be long or dramatic. Simple acknowledgement of God's presence shifts awareness.

Prayer interrupts isolation. It brings desire into the light. It invites assistance rather than self-management. Over time, prayer becomes associated with relief and clarity.

This does not mean prayer eliminates temptation instantly. It means temptation no longer operates alone.

Prayer restores awareness of God's nearness in moments when hiding feels tempting.

Practical Tools for Protection

Boundaries become sustainable when they are practical and specific. General intentions often fail. Clear tools support consistent practice.

Time-Based Boundaries

Certain times require additional protection. Establishing routines for evenings, mornings, or unstructured hours reduces vulnerability. Sleep, rest, and structure are not luxuries. They are protective.

Planning ahead prevents decision fatigue.

Device-Based Boundaries

Devices are powerful tools that require wise limits. Filters, accountability software, restricted access, or shared passwords can reduce opportunity. These tools do not indicate mistrust. They indicate intention.

Limiting access does not weaken freedom. It strengthens it.

Emotional-State Awareness

Emotional awareness is a boundary in itself. Noticing when stress, sadness, or exhaustion increases temptation allows for compassionate intervention. Addressing emotions directly reduces the need for escape.

Emotions ignored often seek expression through habits.

Boundaries Support Alignment

Boundaries are not the source of freedom. They support it. They create an environment where renewal of the mind can take root and grow.

When boundaries are practiced consistently, temptation loses control. Choices regain space. Awareness remains active.

Boundaries do not exist to shame failure. They exist to protect progress.

Freedom is not maintained by strength alone.
It is maintained by wisdom.

Reflection

1. What times or situations increase vulnerability most often?
2. How does the environment influence attention and choices?
3. What forms of strategic resistance feel realistic for you?
4. How might immediate prayer change moments of temptation?
5. What boundaries could be reframed as protection rather than punishment?

Chapter 10 The Gift of Accountability

*"Confess your sins to one another and pray for
one another, that you may be healed."*
(James 5:16, ESV)

Core Truth: Healing accelerates in a trusted community.

Why Isolation Feeds Addiction

Addiction grows best in isolation. This is not because people
are weak, but because secrecy removes resistance. When
struggles are hidden, it is no longer challenged by truth,
encouragement, or shared perspectives. The mind becomes
the only voice in the room.

Isolation amplifies distortion. Thoughts go untested. Shame
goes unchecked. Temptation feels louder because nothing
interrupts it. Over time, isolation convinces people that they
are alone in their struggle, even when they are surrounded by
others.

This is why pornography thrives in secrecy. It offers privacy
without relationship and relief without exposure. Isolation
becomes both the environment and the fuel.

Community disrupts this pattern. The moment the struggle is spoken, its power diminishes. Light weakens what secrecy strengthens.

What Accountability Is and Is Not

Accountability is often misunderstood, and that misunderstanding keeps people from embracing it. Many associate accountability with monitoring, interrogation, or punishment. That version of accountability creates fear, not freedom.

True accountability is relational, not regulatory. It is not about control. It is about alignment. It exists to support growth, not to enforce compliance.

Accountability is not:

- Surveillance
- Shaming
- Constant reporting
- A replacement for personal responsibility

Accountability is:

- Shared honesty
- Mutual encouragement
- Truth spoken with grace

- Support during vulnerability

Healthy accountability creates a space where honesty is safe, and progress is celebrated. It invites people out of hiding without fear of condemnation.

Removing Shame From Confession

Confession is meant to be a doorway to healing, not a sentence of guilt. When confession is paired with shame, people learn to hide rather than to heal. When it is paired with grace, honesty becomes possible.

Shame says, You are your struggle.
Grace says, You are more than your struggle.

Removing shame from confession does not mean minimizing sin. It means addressing it without attaching identity to failure. Confession becomes a practice of truth rather than self-punishment.

In safe accountability relationships, confession is met with listening rather than shock, prayer rather than judgment, and encouragement rather than control. This environment allows people to stay engaged even when progress is slow.

Healing accelerates where shame loses its voice.

Choosing Safe and Mature Accountability Partners

Not every relationship is suited for accountability. Wisdom is required in choosing who to invite into this space. A safe accountability partner is not perfect, but they are mature, trustworthy, and grounded.

Healthy accountability partners:

- Are emotionally stable
- Can listen without reacting
- Maintain confidentiality
- Speak truth without condemnation
- Pursue their own growth

They are not fixers or enforcers. They are companions. The goal is not to be policed, but to be supported.

Accountability works best when it is mutual. Shared pursuit builds trust. Shared vulnerability deepens connection. Healing becomes a collective journey rather than a solitary burden.

Accountability as a Shared Pursuit

It is important to state this clearly.

Accountability is not surveillance.
It is a shared pursuit of freedom.

In a shared pursuit, success is celebrated, setbacks are processed honestly, and progress is measured over time rather than by perfection. The focus remains on alignment rather than behavior alone.

A shared pursuit keeps people moving forward even when the path is uneven. It replaces isolation with presence and fear with support.

God designed healing to occur in community. Not because individuals are incapable, but because the relationship reflects His nature. Freedom is not meant to be carried alone.

Walking Together in the Light

Inviting accountability is an act of courage. It requires trust. It requires humility. But it also opens the door to sustained healing.

When struggles are shared, they no longer define identity. When honesty is practiced, awareness remains intact. When community is present, isolation loses its grip.

This chapter completes a significant shift in the book. You have moved from silence to awareness, from isolation to connection. The chapters ahead will focus on living restored, maintaining alignment, and walking forward without a shame identity.

Freedom is strengthened when it is shared.
Healing accelerates when it is supported.

Reflection

1. In what ways has isolation increased the weight of
    your struggles?
2. How have you previously understood accountability?
3. What fears surface when you consider inviting
    someone into this space?
4. What qualities would make an accountability
    relationship feel safe?
5. How does reframing accountability as a shared pursuit
    change your willingness to engage?

Chapter 11 Restored Identity and Intimacy

"For freedom Christ has set us free; stand firm therefore."
(Galatians 5:1, ESV)

Core Truth: Freedom is not the absence of temptation, but the restoration of alignment.

Freedom Redefined

Many people define freedom as the complete absence of temptation. When temptation returns, they assume something is wrong or that progress has been lost. Scripture offers a different understanding.

Freedom is not the elimination of desire. It is the reordering of desire. Alignment means that temptation no longer holds authority. It may appear, but it does not define direction.

Restored identity is marked by stability rather than instability. When identity is rooted in alignment with God, occasional temptations do not collapse confidence. The heart remains oriented toward what is life-giving.

Freedom is sustained by awareness, not perfection.

Relearning Intimacy

Intimacy often needs to be relearned after pornography has shaped expectations. This process is not rushed. It unfolds through patience, presence, and trust.

Relearning intimacy involves slowing down. It values connection over performance and presence over outcome. Intimacy becomes an exchange rather than an experience to consume.

For some, this means learning to be emotionally available again. For others, it involves rebuilding comfort with vulnerability. This relearning is gentle and progressive.

Intimacy grows where safety and honesty are practiced consistently.

Rebuilding Trust

Trust is rebuilt through consistency rather than declarations. Words may begin the process, but actions sustain it. Small, repeated choices create credibility over time.

This applies both relationally and internally. Trust with others grows as boundaries are honored and accountability is maintained. Trust in oneself grows as alignment becomes dependable.

Rebuilding trust does not mean ignoring the past. It means learning from it without living under its shadow. Growth is measured by trajectory rather than flawlessness.

Trust is restored where honesty remains constant.

Healing the Imagination

The imagination is a powerful formative space. Pornography trains imagination towards fantasy detached from reality. Healing involves retraining the imagination towards truth and connection.

This retraining happens through intentional focus. What the mind rehearses shapes what the heart desires. Scripture, prayer, creativity, and a healthy relationship provide new material for the imagination.

Healing the imagination does not mean suppressing thoughts forcefully. It means replacing them with richer, truer images. Over time, old images lose clarity and influence.

The imagination heals where attention is redirected consistently.

Living Without a Shame Identity

Shame attempts to define identity by past behavior. It whispers that failure is permanent and that progress is fragile. Restored identity resists this narrative.

Identity rooted in Christ is not erased by struggles. It is strengthened by dependence. When shame is rejected, honesty becomes sustainable.

Walking forward without a shame identity means acknowledging growth without fear of relapse, defining worth. It means responding to temptations with awareness rather than panic.

Freedom matures when identity remains anchored.

A Life of Alignment

Restored identity and intimacy are not endpoints. They are ongoing realities maintained through awareness, community, and alignment. This life is not marked by fear of failure, but by confidence in God's nearness.

As alignment deepens, temptation loses urgency.

- Desire becomes integrated.

- Relationships become richer.

- Awareness remains active.

Freedom is not fragile.
It is cultivated.

Reflection

1. How have you previously defined freedom?
2. What might relearning intimacy require in this season?
3. Where does trust need to be rebuilt gradually?
4. How has your imagination shaped desires in the past?
5. What does walking without a shame identity look like practically?

Chapter 12 Living Free and Staying Aware

"If we walk in the light, as he is in the light, we have fellowship with one another."
(1 John 1:7, ESV)

Core Truth: Freedom is maintained through presence, not perfection.

Freedom Is Sustained, Not Achieved

Many people approach freedom as a destination. They imagine a future moment when the struggles no longer exist, and temptations disappear. When that moment does not arrive, discouragement follows.

Scripture presents freedom differently. Freedom is not a finish line. It is a way of living that is sustained through relationship. It grows through dependence rather than self-sufficiency.

Living free does not mean never feeling tempted. It means temptation no longer defines identity or direction. The heart remains oriented towards God even when desire fluctuates. Awareness stays intact.

Freedom matures as presence becomes habitual.

Ongoing Dependence on God

Dependence is not weakness. It is being in alignment with God. Human strength was never meant to operate independently from God's presence. When dependence is rejected, pressure increases. When dependence is embraced, peace follows.

Ongoing dependence looks like daily awareness rather than dramatic moments. It involves simple prayer, honest acknowledgment, and continued surrender. It trusts that God's grace is sufficient for today, not just for crises.

This posture removes panic from temptation. Instead of responding with fear or self-condemnation, the heart responds with connection.

Dependence keeps freedom relational.

Awareness Versus Fear

Fear is a poor guardian of freedom. It creates vigilance without peace and effort without rest. Fear focuses attention on failure rather than on God's presence.

Awareness functions differently. Awareness notices thoughts, emotions, and patterns without judgment. It remains attentive without becoming anxious. Awareness allows for responses rather than reactions.

Living free requires awareness, not obsession. It means noticing vulnerability early and responding gently. It means choosing presence over avoidance.

Fear isolates. Awareness connects.

Growth Without Condemnation

Condemnation stalls growth. It convinces people that failure defines identity and that progress is fragile. Grace invites growth by removing the fear of rejection.

Growth without condemnation recognizes that healing is rarely linear. Progress includes setbacks. Alignment deepens through consistency rather than perfection.

When condemnation is absent, honesty becomes sustainable. When honesty is sustained, healing continues.

Grace does not excuse sin. It empowers transformation.

Living in the Light Daily

Living in the light is not a one-time decision. It is a daily posture. It involves openness with God, honesty with a trusted community, and alignment of attention.

Light does not eliminate struggles instantly. It removes isolation. It keeps awareness alive. It ensures that temptation does not operate unseen.

Daily living in the light includes:

- Honest prayer
- Continued accountability
- Practiced boundaries
- Intentional renewal of the mind

These practices are not burdens. They are supporters. They protect freedom by keeping alignment central.

Light sustains what secrecy destroys.

A Life Marked by Presence

This journey began by naming silence and ends by embracing presence. Freedom is not found in striving harder or managing behavior more tightly. It is found in remaining aware of God's nearness.

Presence changes how struggles are experienced. It replaces fear with trust, isolation with connection, and shame with truth.

Living free is not about proving strength. It is about remaining aligned.

Freedom is not fragile.
It is maintained through presence.

Final Reflection

1. How has your understanding of freedom changed through this journey?
2. What does daily dependence on God look like for you?
3. Where might fear be replacing awareness?
4. How can grace reshape the way you view growth?
5. What practices help you remain in the light consistently?

Closing Word

If you have read this far, something important is already true. You have chosen honesty over hiding and presence over isolation. That choice matters.

Freedom is not behind you or ahead of you. It is practiced now, one moment of awareness at a time.

God is not waiting for you to arrive at perfection. He is present with you in the process.

Walk forward without fear.
Remain aware.
Live free.

Continuing the Journey

Want to go Deeper?

Additional guided resources are available to help you apply and sustain what God has begun.

Scan the code below to continue the journey.

Or visit: www.calebperkinsministries.com/books

12-Session Study Guide
Walking in Freedom Together

Guiding Principle:
Participation never requires disclosure. Sharing is always optional. Passing is always acceptable.

Before You Begin (Leader & Group Agreements)

- Confidentiality is expected and protected
- No graphic detail, ever
- No fixing, diagnosing, or advising
- Speak from personal reflection, not comparison
- Everyone has permission to pass

Session 1 – Naming the Silence

Based on Chapter 1
Core Truth: Silence empowers bondage.
Purpose:
To normalize the struggle without naming details and to dismantle isolation safely.

Discussion Focus:
- Why silence persists around this issue
- The cost of an unspoken struggle
- Why naming reality matters

Reflection Questions:
1. What stood out to you most in the opening chapter?
2. Why do you think silence often feels safer than honesty?
3. How does silence affect spiritual growth in general?
4. What would it look like to replace silence with light without oversharing?

Session 2 – Understanding the Environment

Based on Chapter 2
Core Truth: Technology is neutral; formation is not.
Purpose:
To remove moral panic and increase awareness of formation.

Discussion Focus:
- Technology as a shaping force
- Accessibility and anonymity
- Early formation and exposure

Reflection Questions:
1. How has technology shaped attention and habits broadly?
2. What surprised you about how formation happens?
3. Why is awareness more helpful than blame?
4. Where might intentional formation be needed today?

Session 3 – How Desire Is Trained

Based on Chapter 3
Core Truth: Repetition reshapes desire.
Purpose:
To reframe struggle as formation rather than failure.

Discussion Focus:
- The brain's reward system
- Habit formation
- Desensitization

Reflection Questions:
1. How does understanding repetition change the way you view habits?
2. Why is shame unhelpful in the formation process?
3. What does retraining desire suggest about hope?
4. How does patience play a role in healing?

Session 4 – The Cost to Intimacy

Based on Chapter 4
Core Truth: What trains the mind weakens intimacy.
Purpose:
To acknowledge impact without fear or diagnosis.

Discussion Focus:
- Expectations versus reality
- Ease versus effort
- Relational presence

Reflection Questions:
1. How does culture shape expectations of intimacy?
2. Why does a real connection require effort?
3. What makes patience difficult in relationships today?
4. How does hope remain central to restoration?

Session 5 – Hiding and Awareness

Based on Chapter 5

Core Truth: God does not leave us; we withdraw from awareness.

Purpose:

To dismantle shame and restore confidence in God's nearness.

Discussion Focus:
- Adam and Eve's response
- Shame versus conviction
- Awareness of God's presence

Reflection Questions:
1. How does hiding affect spiritual awareness?
2. What is the difference between shame and conviction?
3. Why does shame distort perception of God?
4. What restores awareness rather than distance?

Session 6 – Why Behavior Isn't the Root

Based on Chapter 6

Core Truth: Spiritual disorder produces behavioral cycles.

Purpose:

To shift the group from control to alignment.

Discussion Focus:
- Why behavior-only solutions fail
- Formation versus management
- Jesus' method of transformation

Reflection Questions:
1. Why do surface-level solutions often fail?
2. How does alignment differ from control?
3. What does Jesus prioritize in transformation?
4. How does this reshape expectations of growth?

Session 7 – Repentance Reframed

Based on Chapter 7
Core Truth: Repentance is alignment, not self-punishment.
Purpose:
To restore repentance as a hope-filled realignment.

Discussion Focus:
- Biblical repentance
- Willpower limitations
- Renewed vision

Reflection Questions:
1. How have you previously understood repentance?
2. Why does punishment-based repentance fail?
3. What does alignment change about motivation?
4. How does seeing people as image-bearers matter?

Session 8 – Renewing the Mind

Based on Chapter 8
Core Truth: What you behold trains what you desire.
Purpose:
To introduce practical renewal without pressure.

Discussion Focus:
- Prayer as interruption
- Scripture as re-patterning
- Thought awareness

Reflection Questions:
1. How does attention shape desire?
2. Why is interruption more effective than suppression?
3. What role does Scripture play in renewal?
4. What practices foster communion over consumption?

Session 9 – Boundaries That Protect

Based on Chapter 9

Core Truth: Boundaries create space for freedom.

Purpose:

To reframe boundaries as wisdom, not punishment.

Discussion Focus:
- Vulnerable times
- Environmental awareness
- Strategic resistance

Reflection Questions:
1. Why are boundaries often misunderstood?
2. How does the environment influence choices?
3. What makes boundaries sustainable?
4. How do boundaries support alignment?

Session 10 – The Gift of Accountability

Based on Chapter 10

Core Truth: Healing accelerates in a trusted community.

Purpose:

To remove fear around accountability.

Discussion Focus:

- Isolation versus community
- Accountability defined
- Shared pursuit

Reflection Questions:

1. Why does isolation strengthen struggle?
2. How is accountability different from surveillance?
3. What makes accountability safe?
4. Why does healing accelerate in a community?

Session 11 – Restored Identity and Intimacy

Based on Chapter 11

Core Truth: Freedom is alignment, not perfection.

Purpose:

To help participants integrate freedom into identity.

Discussion Focus:

- Relearning intimacy
- Healing imagination
- Living without shame

Reflection Questions:

1. How has your view of freedom changed?
2. What does restored identity look like practically?
3. How does imagination influence desire?
4. Why is shame incompatible with growth?

Session 12 – Living Free and Staying Aware

Based on Chapter 12

Core Truth: Freedom is maintained through presence, not perfection.

Purpose:

To send participants forward with peace, not pressure.

Discussion Focus:
- Daily awareness
- Dependence on God
- Living in the light

Reflection Questions:
1. What practices help maintain awareness?
2. How does presence differ from performance?
3. Why is grace essential for long-term growth?
4. What does living in the light look like daily?

Closing Encouragement

Freedom is not something you graduate from.

It is something you live into.

You are not alone.

You are not defined by struggle.

You are invited to remain aware, aligned, and present.

Scripture for Renewal, Freedom, and Alignment

This Scripture collection is provided for reflection, prayer, and renewal.

You are not meant to read it quickly, but to return to it slowly.

Let these verses reshape awareness, restore truth, and realign desire.

Identity and Grace

"There is therefore now no condemnation for those who are in Christ Jesus."
(Romans 8:1, ESV)

"See what kind of love the Father has given to us, that we should be called children of God; and so we are."
(1 John 3:1, ESV)

"For by grace you have been saved through faith. And this is not your own doing; it is the gift of God."
(Ephesians 2:8, ESV)

"But God shows his love for us in that while we were still sinners, Christ died for us."
(Romans 5:8, ESV)

"He does not deal with us according to our sins, nor repay us according to our iniquities."
(Psalm 103:10, ESV)

Renewal of the Mind

"Do not be conformed to this world, but be transformed by the renewal of your mind."
(Romans 12:2, ESV)

"Set your minds on things that are above, not on things that are on earth."
(Colossians 3:2, ESV)

"Finally, brothers, whatever is true, whatever is honorable, whatever is just, whatever is pure, whatever is lovely… think about these things."
(Philippians 4:8, ESV)

"Create in me a clean heart, O God, and renew a right spirit within me."
(Psalm 51:10, ESV)

"We take every thought captive to obey Christ."
(2 Corinthians 10:5, ESV)

Freedom and Light

"For freedom Christ has set us free; stand firm therefore, and do not submit again to a yoke of slavery."
(Galatians 5:1, ESV)

"If the Son sets you free, you will be free indeed."
(John 8:36, ESV)

"For anything that becomes visible is light."
(Ephesians 5:13, ESV)

"Where the Spirit of the Lord is, there is freedom."
(2 Corinthians 3:17, ESV)

"The light shines in the darkness, and the darkness has not overcome it."
(John 1:5, ESV)

Shame and Restoration

"Those who look to him are radiant, and their faces shall never be ashamed."
(Psalm 34:5, ESV)

"The Lord is near to the brokenhearted and saves the crushed in spirit."
(Psalm 34:18, ESV)

"A bruised reed he will not break, and a faintly burning wick he will not quench."
(Isaiah 42:3, ESV)

"If we confess our sins, he is faithful and just to forgive us our sins and to cleanse us from all unrighteousness."
(1 John 1:9, ESV)

"He heals the brokenhearted and binds up their wounds."
(Psalm 147:3, ESV)

Walking in the Spirit

"Walk by the Spirit, and you will not gratify the desires of the flesh."
(Galatians 5:16, ESV)

"If we live by the Spirit, let us also keep in step with the Spirit."
(Galatians 5:25, ESV)

"Abide in me, and I in you."
(John 15:4, ESV)

"For all who are led by the Spirit of God are sons of God."
(Romans 8:14, ESV)

"Teach me your way, O Lord, that I may walk in your truth."
(Psalm 86:11, ESV)

Closing Encouragement

Scripture renews not through pressure,
but through presence.

Return to these verses when temptation rises,
when shame whispers,
or when awareness feels dull.

You are not striving for freedom.
You are learning to walk in it.

About the Author

Caleb Perkins is a pastor, author, and counselor who has spent years walking alongside individuals and families through deeply personal struggles involving identity, shame, and spiritual formation. His work is rooted in Scripture and shaped by extensive experience in discipleship, pastoral counseling, and ministry leadership.

Throughout his ministry, Caleb has observed how pornography often thrives in silence and isolation, not because people lack desire for holiness, but because they lack safe pathways toward healing. *Hidden No More* was written to address that gap, offering a formation-focused, God-centered approach to freedom that avoids shame, exposure, and fear.

Caleb's writing emphasizes alignment over behavior management, awareness over condemnation, and restoration over punishment. His work is used in individual, counseling, and church settings to help people rediscover identity, intimacy, and freedom grounded in God's presence.

Caleb lives with his family in West Virginia and continues to serve through teaching, counseling, and writing. More resources and information can be found at www.calebperkinsministries.com.